# SEASONS SEASONS SEASONS SEASONS

# SPRING

Moira Butterfield

Illustrated by Helen James

W
FRANKLIN WATTS
LONDON • SYDNEY

 An Appleseed Editions book

First published in 2005 by Franklin Watts
96 Leonard Street, London EC2A 4XD

Franklin Watts Australia
Level 17/207 Kent Street, Sydney, NSW 2000

© 2005 Appleseed Editions

Designed and illustrated by Helen James
Edited by Mary-Jane Wilkins
Tree illustration page 24 Moira Butterfield

ISBN 0 7496 6000 7

A CIP catalogue for this book is available from the British Library

Photographs by Corbis (Mark E. Gibson, Lindsay Hebberd, Steve Kaufman,
Matthias Kulka, Danny Lehman, Joe McDonald, Roy Morsch, Roger Ressmeyer,
Christian Sarramon, Craig Tuttle)

Printed and bound in Thailand

# Contents

# All about spring

Spring is a season, a busy, lively time when animal babies are born and flowers begin to blossom.

The sun gives us life. Without it there would be no animals or plants on our planet.

## Our sun journey

Our Earth travels round the sun, a huge fiery ball of burning gas that gives us our heat and light. It takes one year for the Earth to journey all the way round.

## Earth words

The two halves of the world are called the northern and the southern hemispheres. While one has spring, the other has autumn. The area around the middle of the world is called the equator.

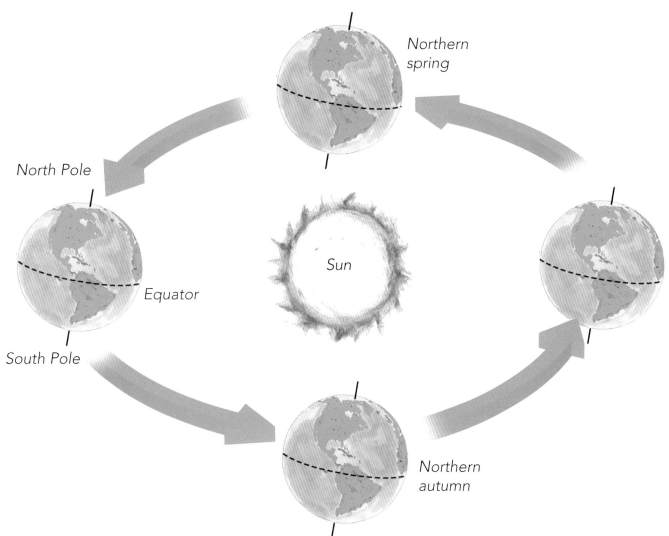

Northern
spring

North Pole

Sun

Equator

South Pole

Northern
autumn

# Here comes spring

As the Earth travels round the sun, the
seasons change. First one half and then
the other half of the planet begins to tilt
towards the sun. Spring arrives for you when
your half of the Earth begins to face the sun
and comes closer to its warming rays.

# Time for changes

Spring is an exciting season because
it brings lots of change. Gradually the
weather grows warmer and warmer,
until finally spring turns into summer.

5

# My spring, your spring

Spring comes at different times around the world. Trees near you might have spring flowers, while trees on the other side of the world are losing their leaves.

## Spring north
In the northern half of the Earth spring comes in March, April and May.

## Spring south
In the southern half of the world spring comes in September, October and November.

## What about the middle?
In countries along the equator it is hot all year round. There is no separate spring or autumn. Near the equator places have wet and dry seasons instead.

## Days and nights

As the Earth travels round the sun it spins in space like a top. It takes 24 hours to spin once. First one side faces the sun, then the other, giving us days and nights. In spring the days grow longer and the nights shorter.

## The big melt

In the far north and south of the world the sea is frozen in winter. Then, when spring comes, the ice begins to melt. It breaks into floating chunks called icebergs. They can be as big as buildings.

*Ships must watch out for icebergs during the spring.*

## Light comes back

The North and South Poles are in darkness for six months of the year, during autumn and winter. When spring arrives they are bathed in daylight again, and it stays light for six whole months.

7

# Spring's coming

When spring arrives the world of animals and plants seems to wake up after a long winter sleep. Here are some spring signs to look out for.

## Listen to spring

Birds start to sing a lot in spring. They are sending messages to other birds like them. They might be trying to attract a mate, or to tell other birds to keep away from their home.

## Smell spring

Lots of trees flower in spring, and the blossom often has a strong perfume. The smell attracts insects that come and feed on the nectar stored inside the flowers.

*Birds sing and trees blossom in spring.*

## Spring gets busy

Spring gradually grows warmer and warmer as the months go by. More and more animals come out. More plants start to grow new leaves and flowers. For nature it is the busiest season of the whole year!

## Busy crawling

When it's warm enough insects hatch and start to crawl around. Worms come up to the surface of the ground, too. They have been hiding deep down in the soil over the winter.

## Busy swimming

Ponds become much more lively places. You might see insects skimming the surface, and midges flying overhead. Frogs lay their eggs, in tiny balls of jelly called spawn.

## Busy building

You might see birds collecting twigs and pieces of grass. They are building their nests, ready to lay eggs and hatch springtime chicks.

9

# Spring weather

In spring the weather grows warmer, but it might not be sunny. There could be rain showers and puddles to splash in. You might even see a rainbow.

## Why does it rain?

1. The sun heats up the water on Earth. Some of the water evaporates, which means it turns into a very fine mist, called vapour.

2. The vapour rises into the air. As it goes higher in the sky, it gets cooler. That makes it change back into water droplets.

3. The water droplets gather together to make clouds in the sky. The droplets gradually grow bigger and bigger.

4. Eventually the droplets are so big and heavy that they fall back to Earth as rain.

Clouds are different shapes and colours. The darkest ones carry the most rain.

Clouds move across the sky because the wind blows them.

## Rainbow season

Rainbows appear when the sun comes out on a rainy day. It shines on raindrops in the air. To see one you need to have the sun behind you.

Sunlight usually looks clear to us, but really it is made up of seven different colours. The raindrops split the light into the seven colours and they appear in the sky.

*Rainbows always have the same seven colours – red, orange, yellow, green, blue, indigo and violet.*

# Spring garden

In spring the sunshine and the rain help plants to begin growing and flowering.

## Why flowers have petals

Inside a flower there are tiny parts for making fruit and seeds. There are also grains of pollen and a store of sweet nectar. The flower petals protect these parts.

## Passing round pollen

A flower needs pollen from another flower before it can grow into fruit and seeds. Insects carry pollen between flowers when they feed on the nectar.

# Why flowers are different

Some flowers are bright and scented to attract insects. Other flowers rely on the wind to blow away their pollen. They are often small and pale.

*Tulips grow from bulbs. In spring many thousands of them flower in the fields of Holland.*

## All about bulbs

Some spring plants grow from bulbs hidden underground. Inside a bulb there is a bud, some tiny leaves and a store of food for the plant.

## Time to flower

When the weather gets warmer the bulb starts to sprout. It uses the food store to grow taller. Its flower grows bigger and starts to bloom in the sunshine.

# Spring farm

Spring is a busy season on the farm. There are crops to plant and new animals to look after.

## Planting season

In winter the ground is frozen hard, but it starts to thaw when spring comes. This is a good time for farmers to plant crops that will grow in the spring sunshine and rain.

## Sowing the seeds

Farmers can plant lots of seeds in the ground using a machine called a seed drill. On small farms in some parts of the world farmers scatter the seed by hand instead.

*A farmer uses a seed drill to sow cotton seeds in California.*

# Come outside!

Farm animals such as cows are often kept inside during winter, protected from the cold. When spring comes and the grass starts to grow, they are taken to the fields again.

## Grass – yum, yum!

Animals that eat plants such as grass are called herbivores. Cows, sheep and goats are all herbivores. They chew the grass and use it to make milk.

## Happy birthday, lambs

Lambs are often born in spring. This is a good time because there is lots of grass for the ewes (mother sheep) to eat. This helps them make plenty of rich milk for their babies.

# Spring animals

Some animals journey to new places, build homes and give birth to new babies in spring.

## On the move

As the weather changes lots of animals migrate. They travel from their winter home to a new home where they can find food and warmth in spring and summer.

## Look up

In spring some birds fly thousands of kilometres from their winter homes to their summer ones. Look out for flocks crossing the skies. They are a signal that spring is here!

## Amazing monarchs

Some insects migrate in spring. Millions of monarch butterflies make an amazing journey from Mexico to the American Great Lakes. On the way they lay eggs and die. When the eggs hatch the new butterflies finish the journey.

## Stay away!

Birds build their nests to try to keep egg-eating enemies away. They make it hard for enemy raiders by building nests high in trees, on steep cliffs or in hidden burrows.

*A huge flock of sea birds gathers in a bay in Alaska, North America.*

## Springtime crowds

In spring sea birds often gather in huge groups called colonies to build nests and lay eggs. Many thousands of birds arrive at the same nesting sites every year.

# Spring babies

Many animal babies are born in spring when it is warm and there is lots of food to eat.

## All kinds of eggs

Birds lay eggs in spring. Wild bird eggs are often speckled so they blend into the background. That makes it harder for egg-eating enemies to spot them.

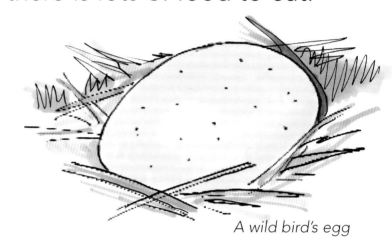

*A wild bird's egg*

*A frog's eggs, called frogspawn.*

## Sea babies

In spring lots of sea animals spawn, which means they lay tiny eggs. Some crabs crawl from the sea to the beach and lay hundreds of eggs that wash into the sea and hatch.

## River babies

Fish eggs hatch in rivers and lakes. The tiny babies are called fry. Frogspawn also hatch into tadpoles. Lots of the tadpoles and fish fry are eaten by other creatures, but some survive and grow into adults.

*A tadpole hatches from an egg and slowly grows into a frog.*

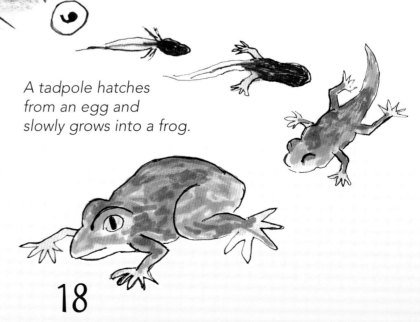

18

## Ice babies

Imagine being born on a chunk of floating ice! That's what happens to baby seals in the far north in spring. The mother seals give birth on the ice chunks to try to protect their babies from hungry polar bears.

## Hungry babies

Female polar bears give birth to baby twins in winter, in a cosy den hidden under the snow. The babies come out for the first time in spring. They follow their mother around as she hunts for food.

*Polar bear babies come out for the first time in spring.*

# Spring stories

All over the world there are legends about springtime. Here are two.

## The myth of Persephone

The Ancient Greeks told many stories about their gods and goddesses. We call these stories myths. This one explains why winter ends and spring begins.

The Ancient Greek goddess of the Earth's plants was called Demeter. She tended the world's crops and made them grow, helped by her daughter Persephone.

One day Persephone was kidnapped by Pluto, the god of the underworld. He took her back to the underworld to make her his wife.

Demeter was heartbroken to lose her daughter, and she stopped caring for the world's plants while she went searching for her. When Demeter found where Persephone had gone she complained bitterly to Zeus, (the king of the gods) and refused to let any plants grow on the Earth.

Eventually Zeus came up with a way round the problem. For three months of the year Persephone had to stay with her husband in the underworld. For the rest of the time she could visit her mother on Earth. When Persephone is away, winter falls on Earth and plants stop growing. When she returns, spring begins and everything starts to bloom again.

# The rainbow and the pot of gold

In Irish legend spring is thought to be a time when fairies are powerful. One type of Irish fairy is called a leprechaun, and legend goes that if you find one he must grant you a wish.

Leprechauns are mischievous, and they have a secret stash of gold. People say that they hide it in a pot at the end of a rainbow. Here is the story.

There was once a greedy old couple living in Ireland. One day the old woman found a leprechaun in her vegetable garden.

"You can have one wish. I'll be back tomorrow to grant it," he said and he disappeared.

When he came back the next day the old couple demanded untold riches, fine clothes, a grand house and all sorts of other luxuries.

"Stop! You are being selfish!" the leprechaun shouted. "I won't grant you anything!"

"But you must! We are poor!" the couple complained.

"All right, I'll give you a clue. I have hidden a pot of gold at the end of a rainbow. If you can find it you'll be rich," the leprechaun replied, winked and disappeared.

The greedy couple rushed out of the house to find the pot of gold, but the leprechaun had tricked them because, however hard you try, you can never reach the end of a rainbow!

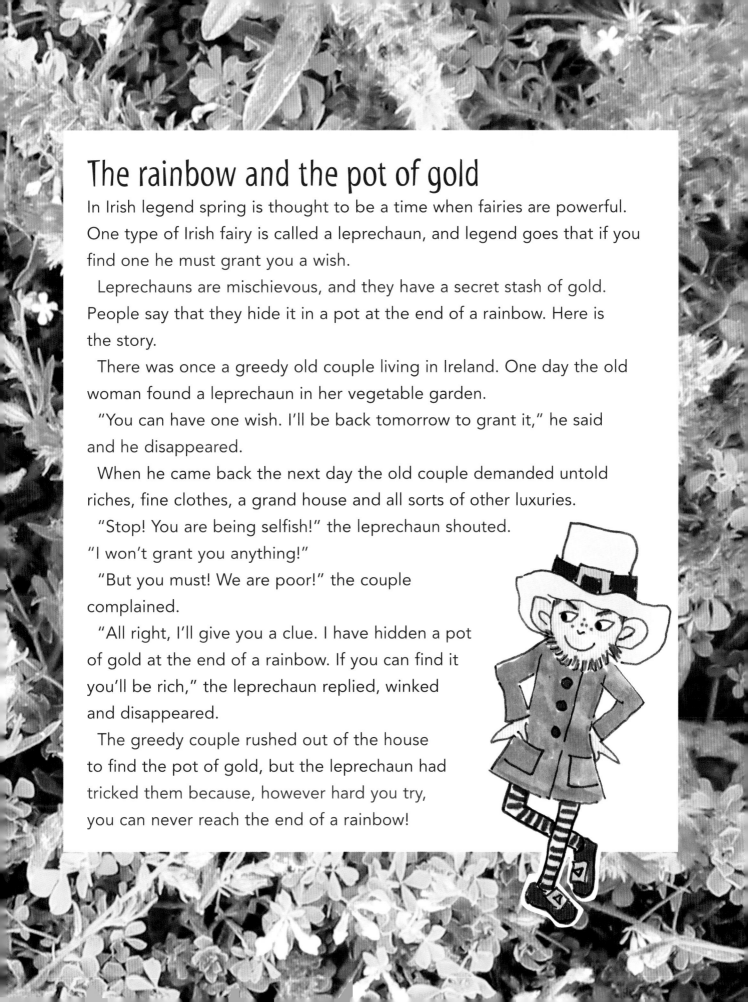

# Spring parties

The start of spring is called the equinox. In the northern hemisphere it falls on 21 March. In the south it is 21 September. People celebrate with parties.

## Hindu Holi

In spring Hindu people celebrate Holi, to thank their gods for the harvest to come. Sometimes it's called the festival of colours because people have fun splashing coloured water everywhere and painting themselves with bright paint powder. There are big processions and bonfires. People throw coconuts and wheat into the fire for their gods and goddesses.

## Spring stars

The Pleiades stars arrive in the northern sky in spring, and Native American tribes hold feasts. Cherokee Indian legend says that the seven stars are seven boys who changed into stars when their mother punished them for being naughty.

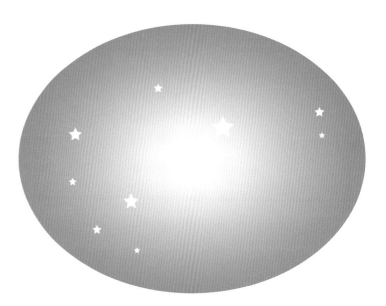

## Bun bang fai

In Northern Thailand, in a place called Amphor Muang, people celebrate Bun Bang Fai in spring. Bun Bang Fai means rocket festival. Local people launch giant home-made bamboo rockets, hoping to shake up the sky so the monsoon rains will start and help their rice to grow.

## Spring snake

The northern spring equinox is special at Chichén Itzá in Mexico. The afternoon sun casts a moving shadow on the wall of the old Mayan pyramid of El Castillo. The temple is built so the shadow-shape of the Mayan snake-god Kukulcán seems to slither down the side of the pyramid to a sacred spot at the bottom.

# Paint the spring

Here are some ideas for making spring pictures.

## Make your picture pastel

In spring lots of flowers blossom in soft pastel colours.
You can make pastel shades by mixing colours with white.
Pale pink, pale blue and pale yellow are all pastels.

## Blossom picture

In Japan the spring cherry blossom is famous for its beauty. Paint a flowering tree on dark paper so that the flowers stand out.
First paint a trunk and some branches. Then add blobs of pale pink for the blossom.

# Spring field

Here are some tips for painting a field
of spring flowers.

1. Paint two-thirds of your paper pale
green. Let it dry, then paint the sky
along the top in a pale colour.

2. When the sky is dry, paint in two hedges, one
along the back of the field and one a little way in front.
This will make the field look 3D.

3. Use red, white, blue and yellow dots of
different sizes to represent flowers in the field.
The flower dots nearest the front should be
bigger than the flowers at the back.

4. Put some tiny sheep at the
back of the field, behind the
first hedgerow. They will help
to give your picture depth.

# Make a piece of spring

Make an Easter egg basket or a spring flower.

## Easter egg basket

Eggs are symbols of Easter, the Christian spring festival. Make a pretty basket and put some chocolate eggs inside for an Easter gift. You will need tracing paper, stiff coloured paper, a ruler, pencil, scissors, and glue or sticky tape.

1. Trace over the basket template on this page. Transfer the shape to the coloured paper and cut it out.

2. Fold along the dotted lines and glue or tape the basket together. Decorate it any way you like.

3. Cut a strip of paper roughly 2.5 cm wide and 12 cm long and glue it to the inside of the basket to make a handle.

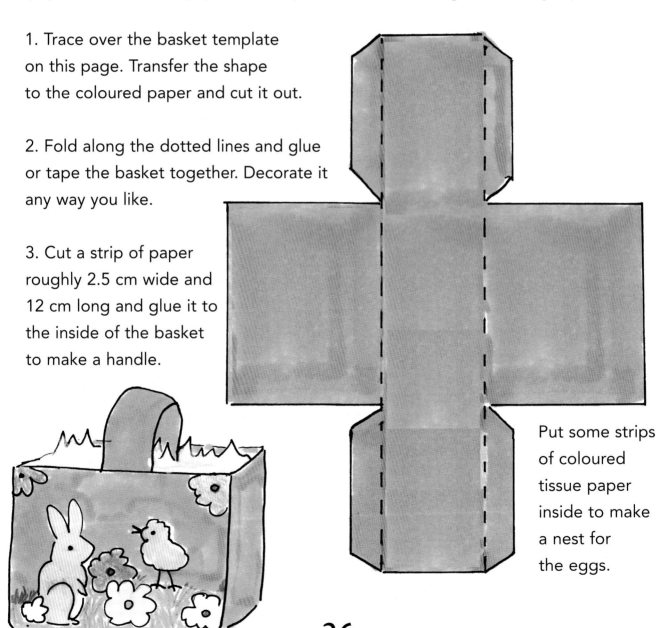

Put some strips of coloured tissue paper inside to make a nest for the eggs.

# Spring flower

Make a pretty spring flower – you could make a bunch and
put them in a vase. You will need a packet of tissue paper,
a pipe cleaner, a ruler and pencil and a cane.

1 Lay eight layers of tissue paper in a
pile. Mark a rectangle roughly 11 cm by
20 cm. Then cut through all the paper
layers, keeping them together in a pile.

2. Fold over one of the long edges
about 1 cm. Then fold it the other way,
and continue, until all the paper is
folded like a concertina.

3. Tie a pipe cleaner tightly round the
middle and wind the other end of the
pipe cleaner round the cane. Gently
open the tissue petals.

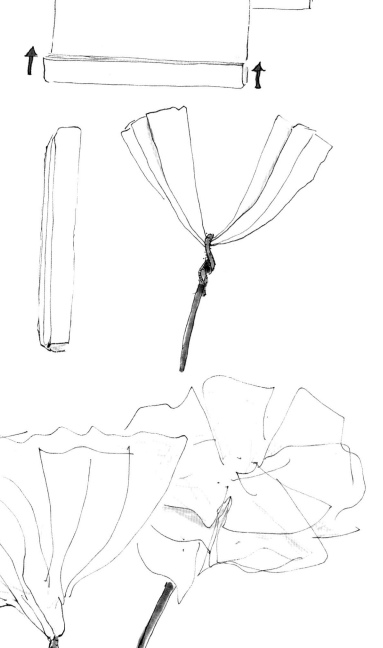

# Be a spring scientist

Discover some spring science by changing the colour of a flower and showing how plants help to make rain!

## Colour magic

When plants start to grow in spring they need water. You can show this by turning a white flower a different colour. You will need a white carnation, a jar of water and some food colouring.

Drop food colouring into the water jar to make it dark. Then put the carnation stem into it.

Before long, your carnation will change colour! That's because plants take up water through their stems. Can you see where the dye has travelled through the petals?

## Go stripy

To make a two-coloured carnation, cut the stem in two lengthwise to about half way up. Put one half in a jar of coloured water and the other half in a jar of clear water. The next day the flower will be half coloured and half white.

# The invisible plant secret

Did you know that plants help to make rain?
Here's how to prove it. You'll need a small pot
plant, a dish, a clear plastic bag and some water.

1. Put the plant on the dish and water it.
Stand it on a sunny windowsill.

2. Gently put the plastic bag over the
plant. Either tie the bag round the stem
or tuck it under the pot.

Look at your experiment
a day later. Has your plant
made any rain?

After a while, the inside surface of the plastic bag will get wet. That's
because plants send water vapour into the air through tiny leaf-holes
called pores. This is called evaporation, and plants all over the world do it.
The water vapour rises into the air, and helps to make clouds and rain.

# Words to remember

**bulb**  A bud, some tiny leaves and a store of food inside a round shape. A bulb can sprout and grow into a plant.

**equator**  The imaginary line around the middle of the Earth.

**equinox**  A time of year when day and night are the same length. There are two equinoxes every year. One equinox signals the beginning of spring and the other begins autumn.

**frogspawn**  Frog eggs inside balls of jelly. The eggs hatch into tadpoles.

**hemispheres**  The northern and southern halves of the world.

**herbivore**  An animal that eats only plants. Cows, sheep and goats are herbivores.

**migration**  A journey some animals make between a summer home and a winter home.

**nectar**  The sweet liquid inside a flower. Insects feed on nectar.

**pollen**  Tiny grains inside a flower. A flower needs pollen grains from another similar flower before it can grow fruit and
sand temperature.

**rainbow**  A curve that appears in the sky when sunlight splits into different colours.

**season**  A period of the year that has a particular kind of weather and temperature.

**seed drill**  A machine farmers use to plant seeds in the fields during springtime.

**spectrum**  The different colours that make up sunlight. They are red, orange, yellow, green, blue, indigo and violet.

**temperature**  How hot or cold something is.

**tadpole**  A baby frog. Tadpoles hatch in spring from frogspawn.

# Index